Sky Watchers

Annabelle Tan

Illustrated by Angeline Drinan

My sister Mary came home.
She had a long box.

"What's that?" I asked.

"It's a telescope, Sam," said Mary.
"We can be sky watchers tonight!"

We took the telescope up to the roof.

"Let's look at the moon," I said.

The moon was gray and bumpy.

"Do people live up there?" I asked.

"People can't live on the moon,"
said Mary. "There's no air or water."

7

"Let's look at a little star," I said.

8

I looked through the telescope.

"The star looks bigger now!" I said.

"Yes, stars are huge balls of gas. They look small because they are so far away," said Mary.

"That star looks red," I said.

"That's not a star," said Mary.
"That's the planet Mars."

"Wow!" I said. "I can see a planet!"

Then a ball of light shot across the sky.

"Sam, look at that!" said Mary.
"That's called a meteor."

"You see amazing things
when you watch the sky," I said.

"Let's come up here every night,"
I said. "I like being a sky watcher!"